WHAT FAMILIES WERE LIKE

THE TUDORS AND STUARTS

ALISON COOPER

Hodder
Wayland

an imprint of Hodder Children's Books

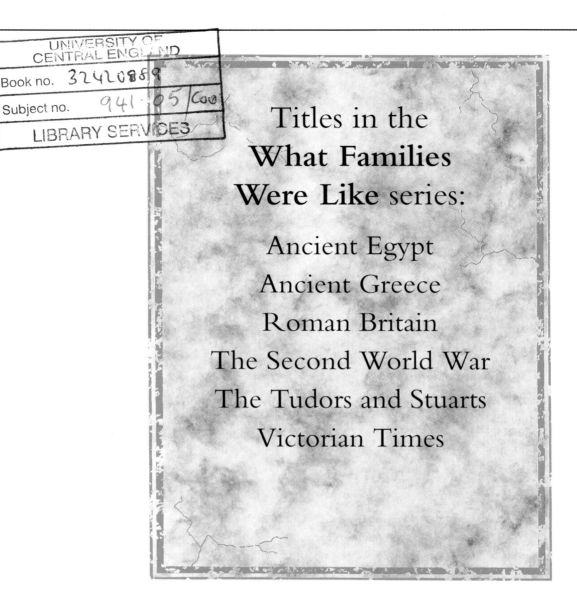

Titles in the
**What Families
Were Like** series:

Ancient Egypt

Ancient Greece

Roman Britain

The Second World War

The Tudors and Stuarts

Victorian Times

This book is a simplified version of the title
Tudors and Stuarts in Hodder Wayland's 'Family Life' series.
Text copyright © 2001 Hodder Wayland
Volume copyright © 2001 Hodder Wayland

Language level consultant: Norah Granger
Editor: Belinda Hollyer
Designer: Jane Hawkins

First published in 2001 by Hodder Wayland, an imprint of Hodder Children's Books.

British Library Cataloging in Publication Data
Cooper, Alison
What families were like - the Tudors and Stuarts
1.Family - History - Juvenile literature
I.Title II.Tudor and Stuart times
941'.05
ISBN 0 7502 3334 6

Printed in Hong Kong by Wing King Tong

Hodder Children's Books
A division of Hodder Headline Ltd
338 Euston Road, London NW1 3BH

Picture acknowledgements:
Cover: pottery figure Christ's Hospital Girls' School, panel painting Longleat House Wiltshire, UK/Bridgeman Art Library, cookery book Pepys Library Magdalen College Cambridge, background woodcut Private Collection/Bridgeman Art Library; B T Batsford 11, 23 (top); The Bridgeman Art Library 18 © Copyright Tichborne Park, Hampshire, 24 top (Forbes Magazine Collections), 27 (top) © Copyright Wilton House, Wiltshire; Christ's Hospital Girls' School 15; English Heritage 22; E T Archive 28 (top); Hulton Deutsch 5 (top), 7 (top), 8, 9 (top), 14, 16 (bottom), 20 (top), 26 (middle), 27 (bottom), 28 (bottom); David MacLeod back cover; Mansell Collection 7 (bottom), 9 (bottom), 12; National Maritime Museum, London 24 and 25 (bottom); National Portrait Gallery 4, 19 (top); National Trust Photographic Library 21, 23 (bottom) © Copyright Lord Sackville; National Trust for Scotland 16 (top); Pepys Library, Cambridge 5 (bottom); Ryedale Folk Museum 10 (top); The Society of Antiquaries of London 19 (bottom); The Tate Gallery 20; Weidenfeld & Nicholson Archives 26 (top right).
All artwork is by Peter Dennis.

CONTENTS

Tudors and Stuarts 4

Farming Families 6

Town Families 12

Rich Families 18

Royal Families 24

Food 28

Glossary 30

Further Information 31

Index 32

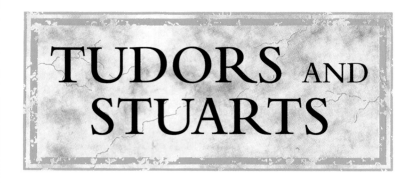

TUDORS AND STUARTS

The Tudors and the Stuarts were two great royal families. Henry Tudor became King Henry VII of England in 1485. His family ruled for over 100 years. His granddaughter, Queen Elizabeth I, had no children. When she died in 1603, her great-nephew became king.

The Stuarts

The new king's name was James Stuart. He was already King James VI of Scotland. Now he was James I of England too.

The Stuart family ruled for most of the 1600s. But in 1642 a war broke out between people who supported King Charles I and people who supported Parliament. The king's side lost and he was executed in 1649. Eleven years later, Charles's son became King Charles II. The last of the Stuart kings and queens was Queen Anne. She died in 1714.

◀ King James VI of Scotland, aged eight.

4

A father teaching his family about religion. There were many new ideas about religion at this time. ▶

Clues from the past

This is what happened to the royal families. But what was life like for ordinary families? Houses, furniture and even books and paintings have survived since Tudor and Stuart times. These give us clues about everyday life. You will find evidence like this as you read this book.

THE
Gentlewomans Delight
IN
COOKERY.

Licensed according to Order.

LONDON, Printed for J. Back, at the Black

◀ Books like this give us clues about the kind of food people ate.

FARMING FAMILIES

In the 1500s and 1600s most people earned their living from farming. They got other useful products from their animals, besides food. Wool from sheep was very important. A lot of it was sold to other countries to be made into cloth.

Farming changes

Until the 1500s, open field farming was used in many areas. There were three large fields around each village. Each field was divided into strips and the strips were shared out between the farmers in the village. Some farmers owned their strips. Others rented them from richer landowners.

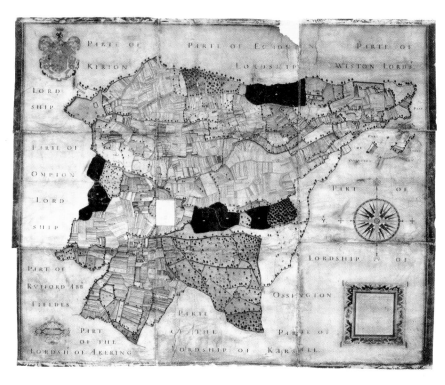

▲ This map of Laxton, in Nottinghamshire, shows the open fields around the village in 1635.

In the 1500s some rich farmers and landowners stopped growing crops. They could make much more money selling wool. They fenced off their land and began to keep sheep instead.

◀ A shepherd looking after sheep, from the *Shepherd's Calendar* of 1579.

Landowners needed a lot of workers to grow and harvest crops, but they only needed a few to look after sheep. Many workers lost their jobs and had to leave their homes. A writer called Thomas More described what was happening like this:

'Poor wretched men, women, children, babes… Away they trudge …finding no place to rest in… What can they do but steal and be hanged or else go about begging?'

This poor family probably had to leave their home when their farmland was fenced off for sheep. ▶

7

Farm work

Farming was hard work. All the family helped on the farm, even the children. Only the children of a few wealthy farmers went to school.

Crops

Farmers grew wheat, rye, barley, oats and beans. They sowed seeds in the autumn or spring. Children used catapults to scare birds away from the seeds. In early summer farmers cut and dried grass to make hay. At the end of the summer everyone worked hard together to bring in the harvest.

Animals

People did not keep animals just for food. Feathers from ducks and geese were used to fill mattresses. Sheep provided wool and their manure improved the soil. This old rhyme shows that they had other uses too:

'Sheep tallow [fat] makes the candles white
To burne and serve us day and night…
His hornes some shepherds will not lose
Because with them they patch their shoes.'

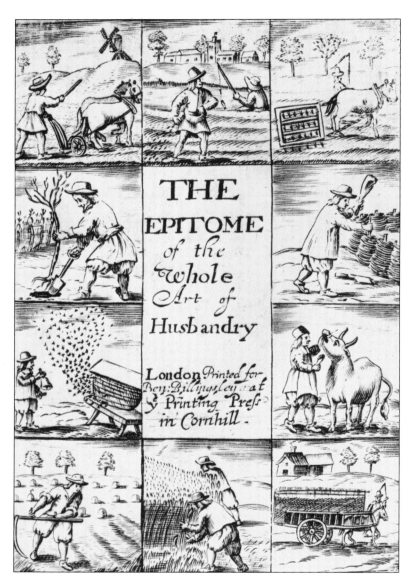

▲ This is a page from a book about farming. The pictures show the many jobs farmers had to do.

Children helped their mothers to look after young animals. They fed chickens and collected eggs. They also watched the animals as they grazed, to protect them and make sure they did not wander off.

▲ These villagers are bringing in the harvest for their landlord.

A May Day dance. May Day was an important celebration. ▶

Farm cottages

Poor farm workers lived in cottages with just one room. Families who owned small farms lived in bigger cottages, with a hall, a parlour and a kitchen. At night the children scrambled up a ladder to a loft over the parlour. They slept on straw mattresses, with sacks of dried peas and bundles of wool piled up around them.

▲ Farmers who were quite well off lived in cottages like this.

The hall might have looked like this. ▼

Farmhouses

Alice Wheatley was the widow of quite a rich farmer. When she died in 1568 she owned a house with a hall, two parlours and a kitchen. It had three rooms upstairs.

These women are shaping cheeses and making butter in a dairy. ▶

Alice's house probably had a dairy, where women made butter and cheese. It probably also had a bakehouse for baking bread, and a brewery where they made ale. There was a garden too. A writer called William Harrison tells us that people often grew 'melons, pumpkins, cucumbers, radishes, parsnips, carrots, cabbages, turnips and all kinds of salad herbs'. Cherries, apples, pears and apricots might have grown in Alice's orchard.

TOWN FAMILIES

In Tudor and Stuart times most people lived and worked in the countryside. Towns were much smaller than they are today. London was a big city though. In 1700 it was the biggest city in Europe. This chapter is about two town families.

▲ These town children are probably playing Oranges and Lemons.

The Shakespeares of Stratford

John Shakespeare was a glove maker and he lived in an English town called Stratford in the mid-1500s. He had spent seven years as an apprentice, learning how to make gloves. Then he had started his own business. Every Thursday he sold gloves made of goatskin and sheepskin in the market.

▲ This is what the Shakespeares' house looked like. John sold gloves from his workshop, as well as at the market.

In 1556 John married Mary Arden. They bought a large house and John set up his workshop there. His business did well. He became an important member of the town council.

In 1564 John's son William was born. This record shows when he was baptised. ▶

▲ Boys in a grammar school in about 1600. A teacher is beating one of the boys.

The Shakespeares' children

John and Mary Shakespeare had eight children, but three of them died when they were young. Their first son was called William. When he grew up, he became an actor and wrote plays. His plays are still performed today.

William and his brothers and sisters probably went to school to learn to read and write. Later, the boys went to a grammar school. Older girls did not usually go to school.

Housework

The boys went to school at about seven o'clock in the morning. The girls helped their mother with the housework. They had a servant girl to help them, too. They spent a lot of time learning how to sew and mend clothes because most families made their own clothes. Washing clothes and sheets was very hard work. They had to scrub and rinse them by hand.

People did not wash clothes as often as we do today. They didn't clean their homes as often either. Instead they spread rushes on the floor to trap the dirt. They sprinkled fresh herbs around to cover up bad smells. When the rushes got very dirty they threw them away and put down new ones.

The end of the day

The boys came home from school at about five o'clock in the afternoon. John closed the shop and they all sat down to have supper. Then John hung a lantern outside to light the street. If they had any food left over, Mary put it outside for the beggars.

Christ's Hospital school taught girls as well as boys. This is the uniform girls wore in Tudor times. ▶

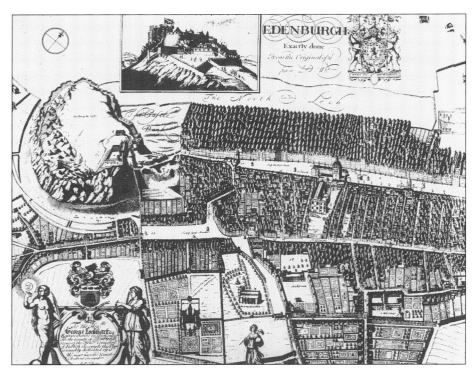

◀ A map of Edinburgh in 1647 showing 'Gladstone's land'.

An apothecary's (chemist's) shop in Holland. There were probably shops like this in Edinburgh too. ▼

The Gladstones of Edinburgh

Thomas Gladstone was a wealthy merchant. In December 1617 he bought a 'land' on the Kings Hie Street in Edinburgh. A 'land' was a tall building made of wood and stone. Lots of people wanted to live in the centre of the city so buildings were crammed together. Thomas, his wife Bessie and their children lived on just the third floor of their 'land'. They rented the other floors out to tenants.

In the cellar, there was a tavern. On the ground floor there were two shops. More families lived in flats on the upper floors of the building. The higher the flat, the cheaper it was to rent.

The Gladstones ate, worked and entertained visitors in their front room. Thomas and Bessie even slept there too. They had a wooden four-poster bed with bright curtains around it. Birds, leaves and flowers were painted on the wooden ceiling. At night, flickering candles cast shadows on the walls.

Their four daughters slept in a separate bedroom. Two servant girls slept on pull-down beds in the kitchen. They helped with the housework – cooking, cleaning and fetching water. They also spun wool and linen on a spinning wheel.

The Gladstones' kitchen looked like this. You can see the servants' pull-down bed on the right. ▼

RICH FAMILIES

Rich families could afford to have paintings made of themselves. Sometimes they wrote about their lives. We can use this evidence to find out what their lives were like.

▲ This is a painting of Sir Henry Tichborne with his family and their servants. It shows the family giving out bread to their farm workers.

John Dee's family

John Dee was a gentleman and a well-known astrologer. In 1578 he married Jane Fromond, who was one of Queen Elizabeth's ladies-in-waiting. He was 50 and she was only 22. They lived in a large house beside the River Thames in London.

The Dees had eight children and John wrote about his family in his diary. You can read some of the entries about his first two children on this page.

1579 JULY
    13 *Arthur Dee born.*
    16 *Arthur Dee christened.*

1580 JANUARY
    16 *Arthur sick with cold.*

    AUGUST
    27 *Arthur was weaned.*
    30 *Wet-nurse Darant was sent away.*

1581 JUNE
    7 *Katherine Dee was born.*
    10 *Katherine was christened.*

    AUGUST
    4 *Katherine was sent home from Nurse Maspely of Barnes because the nurse's maid was sick.*

▲ This painting shows Lady Anne Seymour with her baby son, Henry.

This picture shows a baby being christened in 1624. ▶

Looking after babies

If you look back at the diary entries on page 19, you will see that babies were christened very soon after they were born. This was because many babies became ill and died. People believed that if a baby died before it had been christened it would not go to heaven.

▲ This picture shows the games children played in Tudor times.

Wealthy ladies like Jane Dee did not breast-feed their babies themselves. They had wet-nurses to do this job for them. Some wet-nurses came to live with the family until the baby was old enough to eat food. Sometimes the baby was sent to stay at the wet-nurse's house.

◀ Many mothers died having babies. This mother is showing a new baby to her family but she looks very weak.

Growing up

You can see some of the games children enjoyed playing in the picture on page 20. The Dee children sometimes got into trouble playing.

1590 AUGUST
*   5 Rowland fell into the River Thames over head and ears.*

The Dee children did not spend all their time playing. They had lessons too. When she was nine, Katherine went to live with a teacher.

Girls from rich families learned how to stitch beautiful pictures. This is a cushion cover, from Hardwick Hall in Derbyshire. ▼

Arthur went to Westminster School when he was thirteen. John Dee's sons might have learned arithmetic, astronomy, music, history and geography, as well as French, Latin and Greek. His daughters probably did not learn so many subjects but they had to learn how to do fine needlework and run a big house.

Lady Anne Clifford's family

Lady Anne Clifford was born in 1590. Her family was very rich. In those days rich families often owned several houses or castles. They spent a few months in each one. When they moved house, they took all their clothes, furniture and servants with them. Sometimes children lived in a different house from their parents.

When Lady Anne was 19 she married Richard Sackville, the Earl of Dorset. Their first baby was born in 1614. Her name was Margaret. Lady Anne kept a diary and wrote about her daughter as she grew up.

▲ This is Richard Sackville. He is probably about 19 in this picture. He was the same age as Anne when they got married.

1616 MARCH
> *11 The child had two great teeth come out so that now she had eighteen.*

MAY
> *1 I cut the child's strings off from her coats to get her used to walking on her own. She had two or three falls at first but was not hurt.*

Death and illness

Lady Anne also wrote about Margaret's illnesses.

1616 JANUARY

22 The child had a fit of the ague in the morning. Mr Smith went in the coach to London to my husband to let him know how she was … He came down to see her.

Parents became very worried when their children were ill, because many did not get better. Lady Anne's three sons all died when they were babies. People did not know much about how illnesses were caused in those days and their medicines did not work very well.

▲ This is Lady Margaret, Anne's daughter, aged about 4. She looks very grown up.

◄ This picture from the 1600s shows wealthy children playing.

23

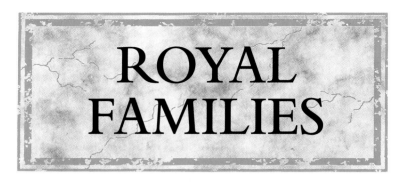

ROYAL FAMILIES

This painting was made in the 1800s. The artist has imagined what the scene would have looked like when King Henry visited his children in the nursery. ▼

Henry VIII's family

When Henry VIII became king he married a Spanish princess called Catherine of Aragon. Henry hoped they would soon have a son who could become king after him. Catherine had six babies, but only one lived. This was a girl, Mary.

Mary lived with her mother for most of the time while she was growing up. Her father loved her but he wanted a son.

Eventually Henry decided to divorce Catherine. Mary's life changed. She was not allowed to live with her mother any more. She was not even allowed to write to her.

King Henry married Anne Boleyn and soon she had a baby – but it was a girl, the Princess Elizabeth. Henry became angry and disappointed. He had Anne beheaded and married Jane Seymour.

A son at last

Jane Seymour did have a son, Edward, but she died just a few days after he was born. Henry married three more times but he had no more children. His sixth wife, Catherine Parr, felt sorry for Mary, Elizabeth and Edward. She tried to make a happier family life for them.

Princess Mary was born at Greenwich Palace in 1516. You can just see the palace on the left in this picture. ▼

The baby king of Scotland

James Stuart was the son of Mary Queen of Scots and Lord Darnley. His father was murdered before he was born and his early life was full of danger.

The artist has imagined this scene showing Mary and James together. ▶

▲ James wrote this letter to Mary while she was a prisoner in England.

James's mother had many enemies who did not want her to be queen. They captured her and forced her to give up her throne. They decided to make James king instead because he was only a baby. He would not be able to rule for many years. In the meantime, they could rule Scotland for him.

Mary escaped from Scotland and fled to England. She was held prisoner there for twenty long years. She sent James many letters and gifts but she never saw him again. In 1587, Queen Elizabeth I of England had Mary executed.

The childhood of Charles II

King Charles I and his wife, Henrietta Maria, were delighted when their first son was born, in 1630. They named him Charles. He had a grand nursery in St James's Palace in London. He had a wet-nurse, another nurse to look after him, and six more ladies to rock his cradle and soothe him.

Charles (left) with his brother James and his sister Mary. ▼

When he was eight, he was given his own court at Richmond Palace. He had seven brothers and sisters to play with.

The happy times soon came to an end. There was a war between King Charles I and Parliament. In 1646 young Charles was sent to France so that he would be safe. In 1649, news came that his father had been executed. Charles had to wait eleven more years before he became King Charles II.

King Charles I and some of his family out on the River Thames. ▶

FOOD

In Tudor and Stuart times, rich people ate good food – and lots of it. At this time people from Europe were beginning to explore faraway countries. They brought back foods and recipes that Europeans had never tasted before. It was a long time before these new foods were cheap enough for ordinary people to eat.

The royal family

Members of the royal family always had a choice of delicious dishes for their meals. Servants prepared the food in a private royal kitchen. Other servants worked in huge, hot kitchens to prepare food for all the ladies and gentlemen of the court.

◄ This painting shows Lord and Lady Cobham and their family eating dessert off silver plates.

Town families

Working families who lived in towns usually had their main meal at midday. Craftsmen closed their shops for a while and children came home from school. They ate roast or boiled meat, or pies, with some vegetables. They might have had fruit or tarts too and a drink of beer, ale or wine. Tea and coffee had not yet been discovered.

These servants are preparing a feast. In the background you can see the guests in the hall. ▶

Farming families

Farming families were usually out working in the fields at midday. They stopped work to eat a pasty, or some bread and cheese. They ate their main meal in the evening. Many families could not afford much food. They survived mainly on bread and pottage, a thick soup.

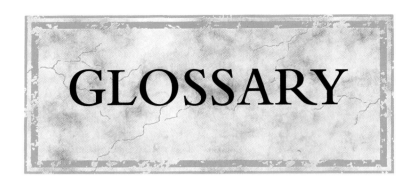

GLOSSARY

Ague A high temperature that makes you feel hot and then shivery.

Ale A kind of beer.

Arithmetic Maths.

Astrologer Someone who studies the movements of stars and planets and how they affect people and events.

Astronomy The study of stars and planets – it is different from astrology because it does not link movements in the sky to events on earth.

Catapult A Y-shaped stick threaded with string, used for throwing stones.

Court A group of rich men and women who looked after a king, queen, prince or princess. The group of people helped to entertain him or her.

Executed Killed as a punishment.

Four-poster bed A bed with a post at each corner. The posts hold up a 'roof' made of cloth and there are curtains around the bed.

Gentleman A wealthy man who was not as important as a lord.

Linen A type of cloth, a bit like cotton.

Merchant A person who buys and sells large amounts of goods.

Parliament In Tudor times Parliament was a group of men who advised the king or queen. He or she could only make people pay taxes if Parliament agreed. In Stuart times Parliament became more powerful.

Rushes Plants with long, thin leaves that grow beside rivers and streams.

Tavern A public house (a pub).

Tenants People who do not own a house but pay money to the owner so that they can live there.

Weaned Given food to eat, instead of just having milk.

Wet-nurse A woman who is paid to breast-feed a baby belonging to someone else.

Books to read

A Day in the Life of a Tudor Criminal by Alan Childs (Hodder Wayland, 1999)
A Tudor Kitchen and *A Tudor School* (Heinemann Library, 1996)
Elizabeth I by Harriet Castor (Watts, 1996)
Look Inside a Tudor Medicine Chest by Brian Moses (Hodder Wayland, 1999)
Mary, Queen of Scots by Harriet Castor (Watts, 2000)

Places to visit

Dorney Court, Dorney, near Windsor, Berkshire, England.
A very handsome Tudor manor house, which has been lived in by the same family for 400 years.

Gladstone's Land, High Street, Edinburgh, Scotland.
A merchant's house, with shops on the ground floor, set up to look as it would have looked in the seventeenth century.

Hardwick Hall, near Chesterfield, Derbyshire, England.
A very big and grand house built by Elizabeth, Countess of Shrewsbury, in the late sixteenth century.

Plas Mawr (Great Mansion), High Street, Conway, Gwynedd, Wales.
A fine Tudor town house, containing many interesting features.

Rydale Folk Museum, Hutton le Hole, Yorkshire, England.
This museum contains farmhouses that have been set up to show what country life was like in the sixteenth and seventeenth centuries.

Traquair House, Innerleithen, Peebleshire, Scotland.
'The oldest inhabited house in Scotland'. Visited by Mary, Queen of Scots, in 1566, it contains several of her possessions, and many other objects from Stuart times.

Welsh Folk Museum, St Fagans, near Cardiff, South Glamorgan, Wales.
Reconstructed farmhouses and farm buildings, including those of the sixteenth and seventeenth centuries.

INDEX

animals 6, 7, 8, 9
Anne (Queen) 4

babies 19, 20, 22, 23, 24, 26
books 5

Charles I (King) 4, 27
Charles II (King) 4, 27
children 7, 8, 9, 10, 14, 15, 16, 17,
    19, 20, 21, 22, 23, 24, 25, 27, 29
crops 8

dairy 11

Edinburgh 16, 17
education 8, 14, 15, 21
Elizabeth I (Queen) 4, 25, 26
England 4

farming 6, 7, 8, 9
food 11, 28, 29

games 20, 21, 23

health 19, 20, 23
Henry VII (King) 4

Henry VIII (King) 24
houses 5, 10, 11, 13, 16, 17, 22
housework 15, 17

James I and VI (King) 4, 26

London 12

Mary (Princess of England) 24, 25
Mary (Queen of Scots) 26

religion 5
royal families 24, 25, 26, 27

Scotland 4, 16, 17, 26
servants 15, 17, 18, 22, 27, 28, 29
Shakespeare 12, 13, 14, 15
sheep 6, 7, 8
shops 16
Stratford, England 12, 13, 14

towns 12, 13

wet-nurses 19, 20, 27